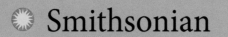
MEGALOSAURUS

by Sally Lee

CAPSTONE PRESS
a capstone imprint

Little Explorer is published by Capstone Press,
1710 Roe Crest Drive, North Mankato, Minnesota 56003
www.capstonepub.com

Library of Congress Cataloging-in-Publication Data

Lee, Sally, 1943– author.
Megalosaurus / by Sally Lee.
pages cm. — (Smithsonian Little explorer. Little paleontologist)
Summary: "Introduces young readers to Megalosaurus, including
physical characteristics, habitat, diet, behavior, and fossil
discovery"—Provided by publisher.
Audience: Ages 4–7
Audience: K to grade 3.
Includes index.
ISBN 978-1-4914-2130-7 (library binding)
ISBN 978-1-4914-2377-6 (paperback)
ISBN 978-1-4914-2381-3 (paper over board)
ISBN 978-1-4914-2385-1 (eBook PDF)
1. Megalosaurus—Juvenile literature. 2. Paleontology—Jurassic—
Juvenile literature. 3. Dinosaurs—Juvenile literature. I. Title.
QE862.S3L443 2015
567.912—dc23   2014021790

Editorial Credits

Michelle Hasselius, editor; Heidi Thompson,
designer; Wanda Winch, media researcher;
Tori Abraham, production specialist

Our very special thanks to Mike Brett-Surman, PhD, Museum
Specialist for Fossil Dinosaurs, Reptiles, Amphibians, and Fish at
the National Museum of Natural History, Smithsonian Institution, for
his curatorial review. Capstone would also like to thank Kealy Wilson,
Product Development Manager, and the following at Smithsonian
Enterprises: Ellen Nanney, Licensing Manager; Brigid Ferraro,
Vice President, Education and Consumer Products; Carol LeBlanc,
Senior Vice President, Education and Consumer Products.

Image Credits

Getty Images: De Agostini/De Agostini Picture Library, 14 (left);
Jon Hughes, cover, 1, 4 (bottom left), 6–15, 17, 20–25; Science Source:
Sheila Terry, 26 (all); Shutterstock: andrea crisante, 6 (Trex), Anna
Kucherova, 12 (bottom right), BACO, 4 (bus), Chris Hill, 19, (br),
Computer Earth, 30–31, Michael Rosskothen, 2–5, 21 (b), Ralf Juergen
Kraft, 11 (bl), reallyround, 5 (br), Steffen Foerster, 5 (bl), T4W4, 4
(folder), Til Vogt, 23 (b); Thinkstock: Graham Rosewarne, 21 (top left),
John Temperton, 21 (tr); Wikipedia: Ballista, 27, Chris Sampson, 28–29,
Ghedoghedo, 16, Rept0n1x, 18; www.discoveringfossils.co.uk, Roy
Shepherd, 9 (tr), 25 (br)

Printed in Canada.
092014   008478FRS15

TABLE OF CONTENTS

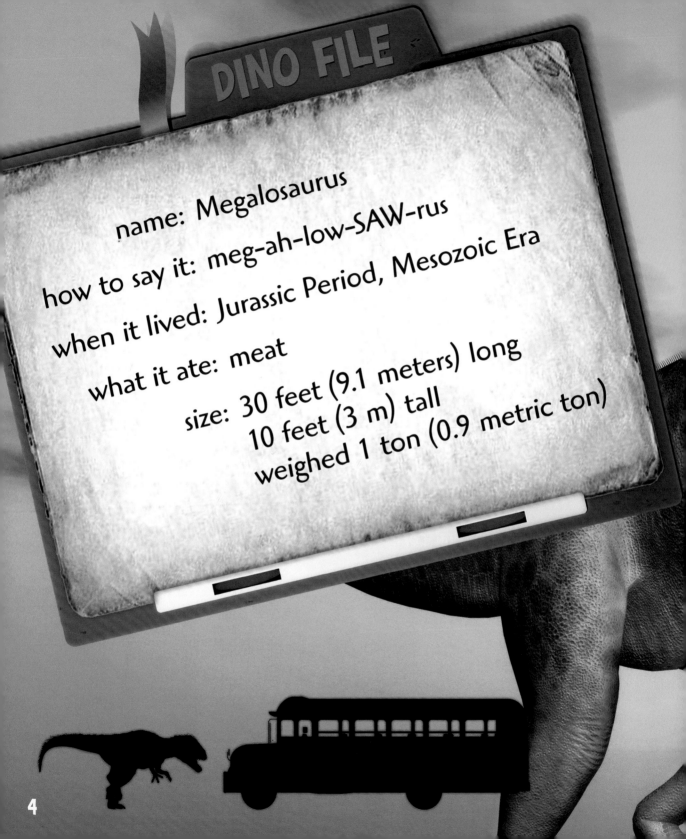

DINO FILE

name: Megalosaurus

how to say it: meg-ah-low-SAW-rus

when it lived: Jurassic Period, Mesozoic Era

what it ate: meat

size: 30 feet (9.1 meters) long
10 feet (3 m) tall
weighed 1 ton (0.9 metric ton)

Megalosaurus was the first dinosaur to be officially named. Before Megalosaurus people did not know dinosaurs existed.

They thought dinosaur fossils were from dragons or giants.

Thanks to FOSSILS

A fossil is evidence of life from the past. Fossils of things like bones, teeth, and tracks found in the earth have taught us everything we know about dinosaurs.

MIGHTY MEGALOSAURUS

heavy tail

long legs

Tyrannosaurus rex

Megalosaurus belonged to a group of dinosaurs called theropods. They were meat-eating dinosaurs that walked on two legs. Tyrannosaurus rex was also a theropod.

large head

curved teeth

small, strong arms

three fingers on
each hand

BALANCING ACT

Megalosaurus had a stiff, bony tail. It helped the dinosaur turn quickly when chasing its prey.

Megalosaurus carried its tail off the ground when it walked and ran. Scientists know this because no tail markings have been found near the dinosaur's fossil footprints.

Megalosaurus footprints found in England

The stiff tail also helped Megalosaurus stay upright. It helped the dinosaur balance its heavy upper body. Without it Megalosaurus would have fallen on its face.

POWERFUL ARMS

Megalosaurus had short arms for such a large animal. But they were strong. Scientists know this from looking at the dinosaur's bones. The arms had large spaces where thick muscles would have been.

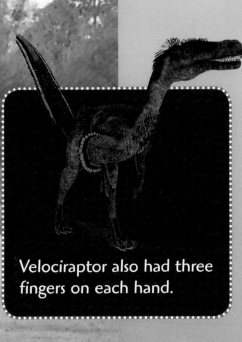

Velociraptor also had three fingers on each hand.

Each hand had three fingers with sharp claws. The claws curved under. Megalosaurus used them to grip or slash its prey.

WALKING TALL

Megalosaurus walked on two strong legs. It had three large clawed toes on each foot. The claws were not used to kill prey. They helped support the heavy dinosaur when it walked.

Megalosaurus means "great lizard." But it didn't walk like a lizard. Lizards walk on four legs that stick out the sides.

Komodo dragon

Megalosaurus also had a small toe on the side of each foot that did not touch the ground.

LIGHT-HEADED

Megalosaurus had a larger brain than many other dinosaurs. Huge plant-eating dinosaurs such as Cetiosaurus were much bigger than Megalosaurus. But their small heads held tiny brains.

Cetiosaurus

Megalosaurus had a
short neck and a large
head. But the dinosaur could
hold its head up easily. Its skull
had many open spaces in it. The
spaces made the skull lighter.

Megalosaurus's powerful jaws
could open wide to take big bites.

JAGGED TEETH

Scientists learned Megalosaurus ate meat from studying its teeth. The dinosaur's teeth were sharp and jagged like a steak knife. They curved backward. This helped Megalosaurus hold wiggly prey in its mouth.

Megalosaurus skull

When Megalosaurus lost a tooth, a new one grew in its place.

HOLLOW BONES

Like other theropods, some of
Megalosaurus's bones were hollow.
These bones made the dinosaur
lighter so it could move faster
than many other dinosaurs.

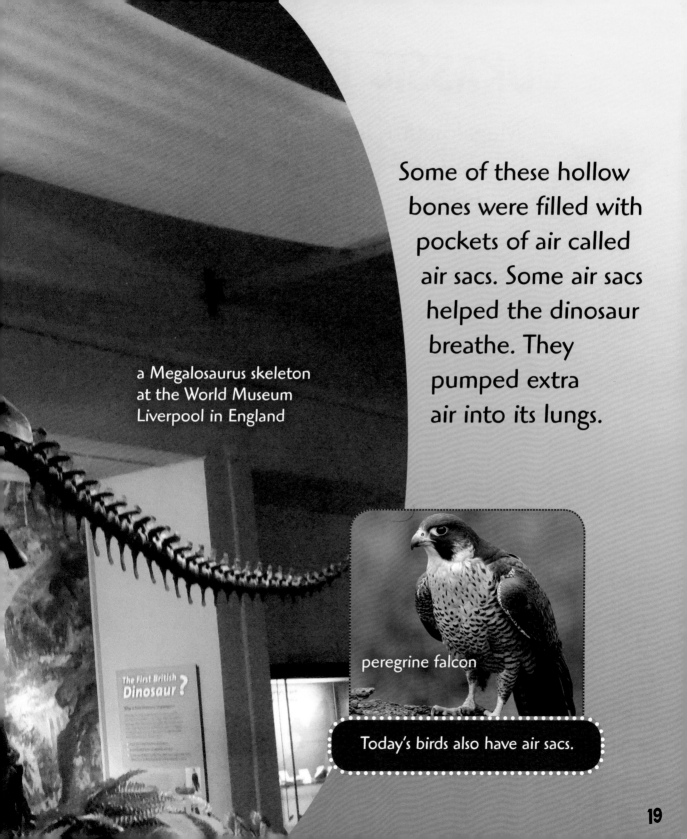

Some of these hollow bones were filled with pockets of air called air sacs. Some air sacs helped the dinosaur breathe. They pumped extra air into its lungs.

a Megalosaurus skeleton at the World Museum Liverpool in England

peregrine falcon

Today's birds also have air sacs.

JURASSIC HOME

Megalosaurus lived during the
Jurassic Period. It made its
home in what is now England.

The Jurassic Period lasted from
200 million to 145 million years ago.

DINOSAUR ERA

TRIASSIC	JURASSIC	CRETACEOUS

| 252 | 200 | 145 | 66 | present |

millions of
years ago

Seas flooded low areas at that time. Palmlike cycads, pine trees, and ferns grew in the warm wet weather. Plant-eating dinosaurs grew large. They gave predators like Megalosaurus more food to eat.

Other Jurassic Animals

Yandusaurus

Huayangosaurus

Shunosaurus

Pterosaurs flew in the air. They were not dinosaurs or birds. Pterosaurs were reptiles with wings made of skin.

Pteranodon was a pterosaur that lived during the Cretaceous Period.

HUNTING FOR DINNER

Megalosaurus was a carnivore.
Carnivores eat meat.
Megalosaurus was a fierce
hunter. It ran fast enough to
grab small mammals and young
dinosaurs. It bit the necks of
large plant-eating dinosaurs.

Megalosaurus was also a scavenger. It ate dead animals and what was left over from another dinosaur's kill. Megalosaurus may have also eaten fish and other sea animals that washed up on shore.

lion

Scientists can guess how dinosaurs hunted by looking at how meat-eating animals hunt today.

LEARNING FROM TRACKWAYS

Trackways are sets of prehistoric footprints found in rocks. They give scientists clues about how dinosaurs moved and lived.

" ... these animals weren't lumbering beasts. They were much more agile than some people have imagined."
—paleontologist Julia Day

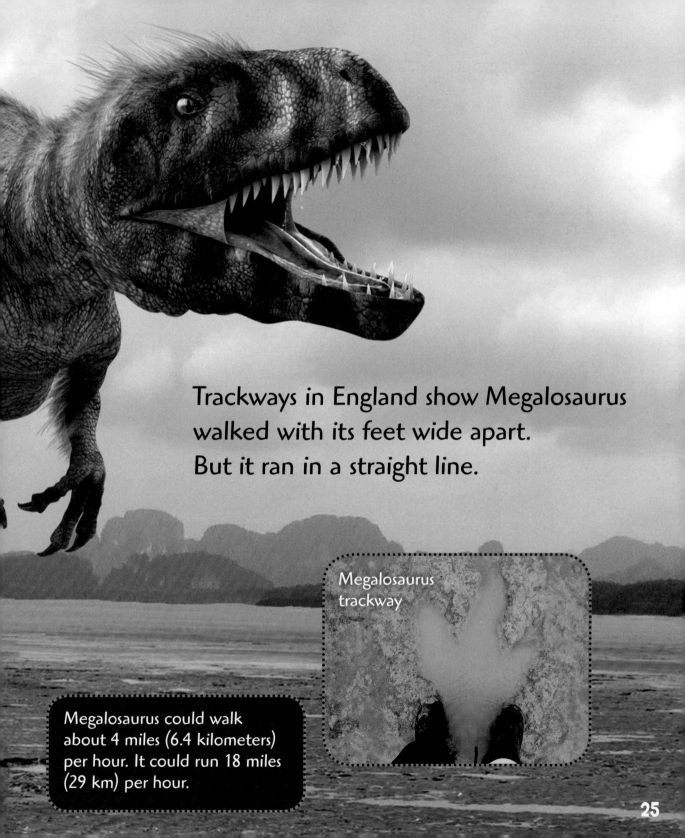

Trackways in England show Megalosaurus walked with its feet wide apart. But it ran in a straight line.

Megalosaurus trackway

Megalosaurus could walk about 4 miles (6.4 kilometers) per hour. It could run 18 miles (29 km) per hour.

STARTING IT ALL

In the early 1800s, geologist William Buckland studied fossils that were found in England. The fossils were too large to be from an animal that lived during his time. Buckland thought the bones belonged to a giant prehistoric monitor lizard.

William Buckland

Buckland named the fossils Megalosaurus in 1824. But he didn't call it a dinosaur. Richard Owen didn't invent the word "dinosaur" until 1842.

Richard Owen

Megalosaurus
The First Dinosaur

The first described dinosaur, from anywhere in the world, was found in Oxfordshire. It was a 9 metre long carnivore that stood on its hind legs; we now call it *Megalosaurus bucklandi*, which means "Buckland's giant-lizard".

The first published record of a dinosaur bone was in Dr Robert Plot's 1677 book *The Natural History of Oxfordshire*. Recognisable today as part of a single thigh bone of *Megalosaurus*, it was collected from 168 million year old Jurassic rocks from Cornwell, near Oxford. Plot wondered if it could have come from an elephant brought to Britain by the Romans, but finally concluded it was the petrified bone of a giant.

A tooth of *Megalosaurus* from Stonesfield, a village 9 miles NW of Oxford, was described in 1699, but it was not until the early 1800s that William Buckland (see case 5) collected from Stonesfield the partial bones displayed here although he also did not know what kind of animal they came from. With the end of the Napoleonic Wars (1815), contact between English and French scientists was renewed and in 1818 the great French comparative anatomist Georges Cuvier (1769–1832) visited Oxford. He examined the Stonesfield bones belonging to an animal resembling a lizard.

Following Cuvier's visit, Buckland started describing the fossils in earnest and he published an account of them in the *Transactions of the Geological Society* in 1824 with beautiful illustrations by his wife Mary Morland.

Finally in 1842, Richard Owen, Professor at the Royal College of Surgeons in London, completed a review of all British fossil reptiles and recognised that *Megalosaurus* together with *Iguanodon* ...

osaurs live?

Most of the Megalosaurus bones Buckland
studied are displayed at the Oxford University
Museum of Natural History in England.

At first scientists thought many fossils
belonged to Megalosaurus. Most of them
turned out to be from other dinosaurs.

GREAT LIZARD ON DISPLAY

Megalosaurus was one of the first full-sized dinosaur models ever built. It was part of a famous exhibit in England in 1854.

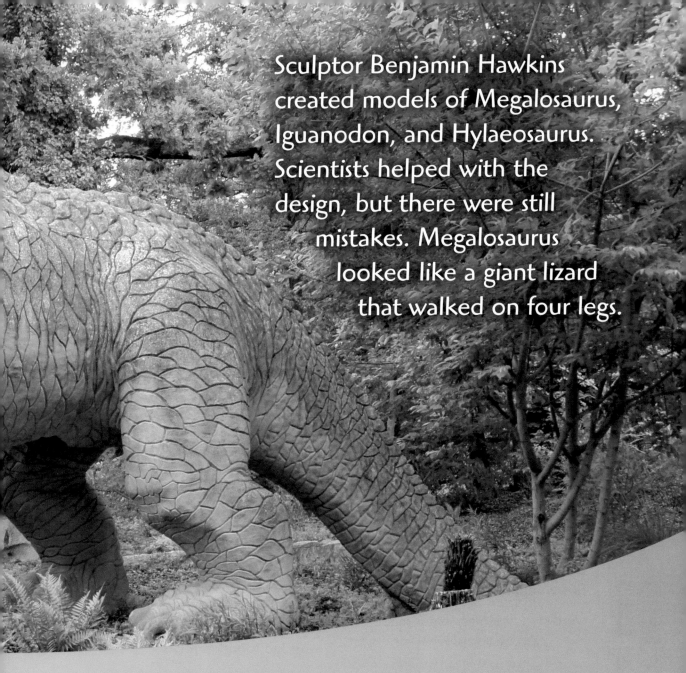

Sculptor Benjamin Hawkins created models of Megalosaurus, Iguanodon, and Hylaeosaurus. Scientists helped with the design, but there were still mistakes. Megalosaurus looked like a giant lizard that walked on four legs.

The dinosaur exhibit made many people aware of dinosaurs for the first time. The Megalosaurus model is still on display in London, England.

GLOSSARY

air sac—an air-filled space in the body that helps an animal breathe and control temperature; birds have air sacs

cycad—a plant shaped like a tall pineapple with palmlike leaves

exhibit—a display that shows or tells people about a certain subject

exist—to live

famous—well known to many people

fossil—evidence of life from the geologic past

geologist—a scientist who studies rocks to learn how the earth has changed over time

Mesozoic Era—the age of dinosaurs, which includes the Triassic, Jurassic, and Cretaceous periods; when the first birds, mammals, and flowers appeared

model—something that is made to look like a person, animal, or object

monitor lizard—a type of lizard found in Australia, Asia, and Africa; monitor lizards eat meat

paleontologist—a scientist who studies fossils

predator—an animal that hunts other animals for food

prehistoric—very old; a time before history was written down

prey—an animal that is hunted by another animal for food

scavenger—an animal that feeds on animals that are already dead

sculptor—a person who creates art by carving stone, wood, or other materials

skull—the set of bones of the head; the skull protects the brain, eyes, and ears

theropod—a meat-eating dinosaur that walked or ran on two legs

trackway—a set of footprints from long ago found in rocks